GW01048691

The Butcher's Daughter
Written by Tommy Watkins

Brutus owned a small butcher shop i
an up-and-coming town.

He had a beautiful daughter named Rachel, who grew up around meat he entire life.

Meat was life, and Meat was king to the butcher.

Rachel met new friends and wanted hang out after school. These new frien were vegan and swore against meat.

Rachel needed to ask her dad if she could hang out with her new friends after school.

Without hesitation, Brutus denied Rachel from seeing these new friends. There will be no vegans around this family! Rachel ran to her bedroom in tears! Brutus's wife Elaine told him it was unfair for Rachel to not meet new people based on their diet restrictions.

After a night of sleeping on his action Brutus woke up and came to have a heart.

He told his daughter she could hang o
with her new friends despite being
vegan.

They could even visit the butcher sho
if they wanted.

Rachel reconciled with her father, went to school that day, and met with her new friends.

The End

Milton Keynes UK
Ingram Content Group UK Ltd.
UKHW050825110824
446741UK00012B/30